D1469648

COMBINES

COMBINES

BILL HUXLEY

Published in 1990 by Osprey Publishing
Limited
59 Grosvenor Street
London W1X 9DA

© Bill Huxley 1990

All rights reserved. Apart from any fair
dealing for the purposes of private study,
research, criticism or review, as permitted
under the Copyrights Designs and Patents
Act, 1988, no part of this publication may be
reproduced, stored in a retrieval system, or
transmitted in any form or by any means,
electronic, electrical, chemical, mechanical,
optical, photocopying, recording or
otherwise, without prior written
permission. All enquiries should be
addressed to the Publisher.

British Library Cataloguing in Publication
Data
Huxley, Bill
    Combines
    1. Combine harvesters, history
    1. Title
    633.1045
ISBN 0-85045-981- 8

Printed in Hong Kong
Page design by Janette Widdows

Many of the photographs used in this book
are of considerable historic interest. In some
case the colour quality is not the same as we
have come to expect from today's film
technology.

Front cover
An International 1460, hard at work

Back cover illustration
*A cutaway view of the Massey-
Ferguson model 38. This machine is
the same as the one used by Phillip
Baker during his record breaking
day's harvesting, described on Page
123. The model 38 is manufactured by
Dronningborg for Massey-Ferguson*

Title page
*The latest Massey-Ferguson 34 and 38
models seen harvesting grass seed in
Hampshire*

For a catalogue of all books published by Osprey Automotive
please write to:

**The Marketing Manager, Consumer Catalogue Department
Osprey Publishing Ltd, 59 Grosvenor Street, London, W1X 9DA**

in the United Kingdom for a big combining unit to gather 3,000 or 4,000 tonnes of grain during a 200–250 working period.

In Southern Europe the harvest is often extended to include maize grain and a single harvester may collect 8,000 tonnes of grain in 600 hours.

By the year 2010 it is estimated that the output from the largest harvesting units will be capable of twice today's capacity.

Engineers and agricultural economists are beginning to rethink the whole process and cycle of combine harvesting. While combines are superb at extracting seeds from their parent plants, it is now recognised that there is tremendous by-product value in crop residues.

It follows, that there are advantages in combines, or machines like combines, gathering the whole crop and delivering it to a barn for processing. This approach is speedier, less energy-intensive, and less dependent upon favourable weather. Should this become the norm then agriculture would have come around a great circle. The earliest binders, after all, where whole crop processors at the barn.

Laurence Rooke

Below
Harvesting at the turn of the century, before threshing machines and combine harvesters became widely available

Getreideernte um die Jahrhundertwende
Harvesting at the turn of the century

Left

The Californian, Benjamin Holt produced the first commercially successful harvesters in the late 1800s. He teamed up with Daniel Best to form what subsequently became the Caterpillar Tractor Company. Numerous other 'firsts' can be attributed to this firm. It pioneered the use of chain belt drives, as an alternative to uncut gears, which had *a tendency to overheat or break if not properly lubricated. It also introduced V belt drives and auxiliary petrol engines. In addition, its machines were the first to have a sidehill harvesting capability. A typical harvester of the period is shown here*

Above

Harris, Brantford open-end binder 1890

EDWARD HUMPHRIES,

AGRICULTURAL ENGINEER AND MACHINIST,

ATLAS WORKS, PERSHORE.

AN ILLUSTRATED PRICED CATALOGUE

SENT FREE BY POST ON APPLICATION.

This Engraving represents one of E. H.'s Patent Prize Combined Double-Blast Finishing Threshing Machines. It is fitted with the Patent Wood Spring Hangers, Patent Expanding Rotary Corn Screen, and all other recent improvements. For lightness, durability, and efficiency, they are not to be surpassed by any in the kingdom. E. H. can flatter himself that he is in a position to supply his customers with a first-class article, having manufactured and sold upwards of 3500 Threshing Machines since commencing business, always using the very best material, and employing first-class workmen only.

E. H. has several good Second-Hand Steam Engines for Sale, 4 to 10-horse power, Cheap.

Left

This oxen powered harvester, in Tunisia, illustrates Massey Harris' widespread coverage of the world market even at a very early stage in the company's development

Above

Edward Humphries was one of the founders of the Fisher Humpries Company. During the nineteenth century he produced this threshing box. Archive material shows that quite a number were sold in the Berlin area

Below
The Sylvester Auto Thresher was a determined, but short-lived attempt, to develop a harvester suitable for the Canadian market during the early years of this century

Clayton

Publication No. C.S. 135

HARVESTER THRASHERS

First in 1852

When Clayton & Shuttleworth constructed and INTRODUCED THE FIRST COMBINED FINISHING THRASHING MACHINE, and for this were awarded the **FIRST PRIZE** at the Royal Agricultural Society's Show at Lewes.

HIGHEST AWARD : SILVER MEDAL.

Royal Agricultural Society of England, Warwick Show, 1931

First in 1928

When Clayton & Shuttleworth designed and constructed

THE FIRST
ENGLISH HARVESTER-THRASHER.

Far left

A Rumely 16 ft combine harvesting flax. The Advance Rumely Company of La Porte, Indiana entered the combine market in 1925 with its No. 1 Hillside model. It continued building ruggedly constructed machines until it was acquired by Allis-Chalmers in 1931. During 1933, one of these machines arrived in the UK for trials. It appears to have coped with British conditions quite satisfactorily

Left

Two years after producing the first combine to be built in the UK, in 1928, Clayton and Shuttleworth went bankrupt. The company was bought by Marshall of Gainsborough who went on to manufacture a large number of combines for use in both Europe and North Africa. At this time, though, it was felt that combines of this particular size, the Marshall had a 12 ft cut, were unsuitable for use in the UK, because of the climate and the relatively small size of the farms

Right
Gebrüder Claas has the distinction of being the first manufacturer in Europe to build a combine harvester. It was a wrap-around model powered by a Lanz Bulldog

Below
The first design produced by Claas was not ideally suited to European conditions. However, after the company recruited Dr Brenner, one of the leading agricultural experts of the time, it soon began to make rapid progress. In 1936 Claas was ready to launch the MDB model; 1,400 were made before the Second World War stopped production

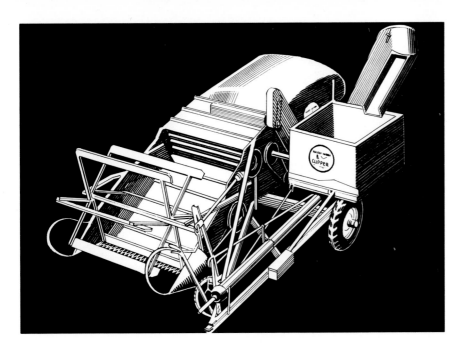

Left
The Massey Harris Clipper, pull-type, and later, self propelled 6 ft and 7 ft cut harvester of 1938. Compact machines such as this soon gained widespread acceptance amongst smaller farmers. To them, the Clipper was an affordable, easy to handle machine which allowed them to harvest their own crops at their convenience

Below
A 1946 prototype from the long established Fahr Company of Gottmadigen. Fahr are now part of the Klockner-Humholt-Deutz AG group of Cologne, West Germany

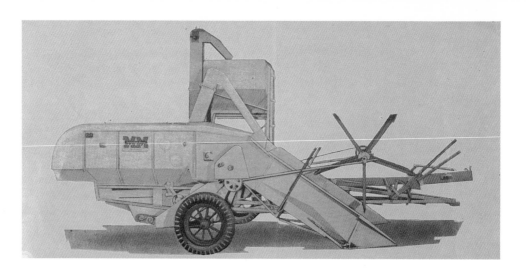

Left
The model 69 greatly enhanced Minneapolis-Moline's reputation and proved to be a very popular machine. When circumstances permit, Henry Flashman, the avid Minneapolis-Moline collector from Cornwall, hopes to add one to his impressive collection of tractors

Below left
This Allis-Chalmers All-Crop 40 was the forerunner of today's trial plot machines. It was converted to self propelled mode, in 1954, by the National Institute of Agricultural Engineering at Silsoe, Bedfordshire. This conversion led to four more being modified by E. Allman and Company, (long time Allis-Chalmers dealers in Sussex, now noted for their range of spraying equipment) to meet the requirements of the National Institute of Agricultural Botany

Below
Australia's involvement in mechanised harvesting dates back to the mid 1800s and the stripper of Messrs. Bull and Ridley. Shown here is the 1901 Sunshine harvester manufactured by the renowned HV McKay Company, which later joined Massey Harris (Massey-Ferguson)

Massey-Harris became associated with H. V. McKay Company in Australia in 1930 and Massey-Harris-Ferguson acquired the company in 1955. Shown is a 1901 machine.

The Sunshine Harvester

SUNSHINE

HUGH VICTOR McKAY MANUFACTURER BALLARAT.

Below
The No. 5 Reaper-Thresher of 1922
embodied a number of then radical
innovations. It was the first Massey
Harris machine to use a petrol engine
to supply operating power, instead of
the more traditional ground-wheel-
drive. It also incorporated a rasp bar
cylinder and concave threshing drum,
as opposed to the peg tooth cylinder
favoured by the Americans. This led to
it being referred to as the 'English
style threshing drum'. The No. 5
Reaper-Thresher was developed for
use in the Argentine as well as North
America. A No. 5 demonstrated its
versatility in 1924 when it successfully
harvested a crop of soya beans in
Illinois

Right
After having produced threshing
machines for many years the Jerome
Increase Case Company of Racine,
Wisconsin, decided to enter the
combine market in the 1920s. Even so,
the company felt it would be wise to
cater for all sectors and continued to
produce threshers for another 30
years. However, its extensive, and
attractive, advertising suggests the
copany had the belief that its new
product had a very promising future

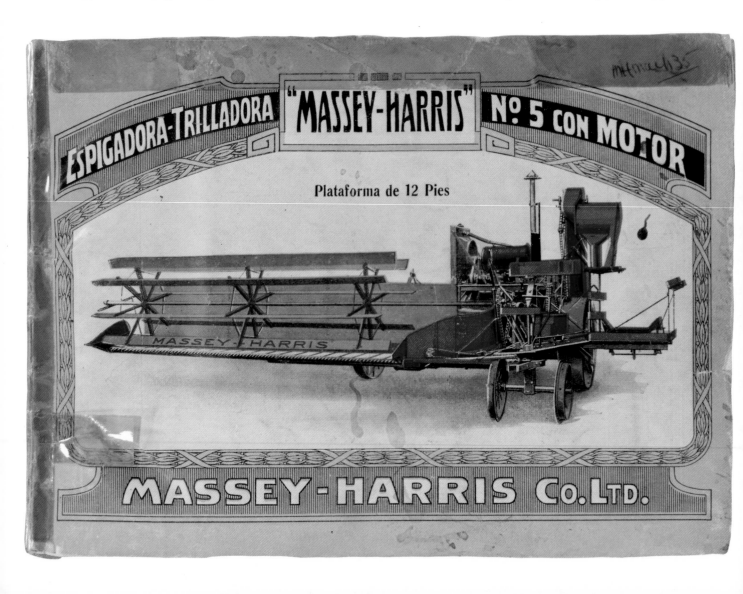

ESPIGADORA-TRILLADORA "MASSEY-HARRIS" Nº 5 CON MOTOR

Plataforma de 12 Pies

MASSEY-HARRIS Co. Ltd.

CASE
COMBINES
Models A, H and P

{ Save Time
Labor
and Grain }

J. I. CASE T. M. CO. INC.
ESTABLISHED 1842
RACINE-WISCONSIN-U.S.A.

OLIVER
NICHOLS & SHEPARD
COMBINES

OLIVER FARM EQUIPMENT SALES COMPANY

Left
*Business prospered after the Nichols
and Shepard Company decided to get
together with the Oliver Farm
Equipment Company. In the late 1920s
the new firm secured a substantial
order from the USSR. Illustrated is a
model D Western Special of the 1930s*

Left
*The John Deere Company first entered
the combine market in 1927. In 1936
it bought the Holt harvester business
from the Caterpillar Tractor Company
which had decided to direct its
resources towards building tracked
and associated vehicles, for the
construction industry*

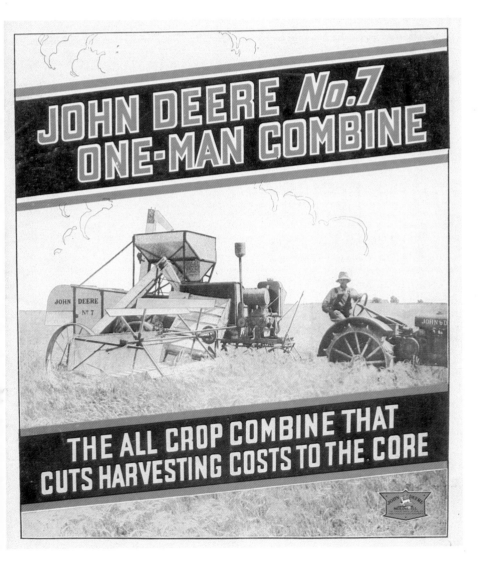

Above and right
On the restoration scene, tractors tend
to overshadow combines and other
farm equipment. Ron Knight of
Stamford, Lincolnshire, however,
takes a pride in restoring all types of
agricultural machinery. This is his
recently restored 1935, IH model 31T
harvester, it is marvellous to see
hitherto neglected machinery after a
thorough re-build. It looks good
externally and the inner workings
have also been restored to the same
pristine condition

Below
Ron Knight's IH model 31T, together with his smaller model 22. Both were obtained from the ex-IH harvester facility in Angiers, France. The 22 still works occasionally

Right
Curtis Baldwin may have been a little inconsistent in his business dealings but some of his ideas were way ahead of their time. Two examples of this were his proposal for a wrap-around combine, which several other companies took up later, and his development of the first American combine corn head. The well known Gleaner Baldwin company of Missouri became the Allis-Chalmers harvester plant in 1955

GLEANER

BALDWIN
COMBINE
12 Foot
Model F

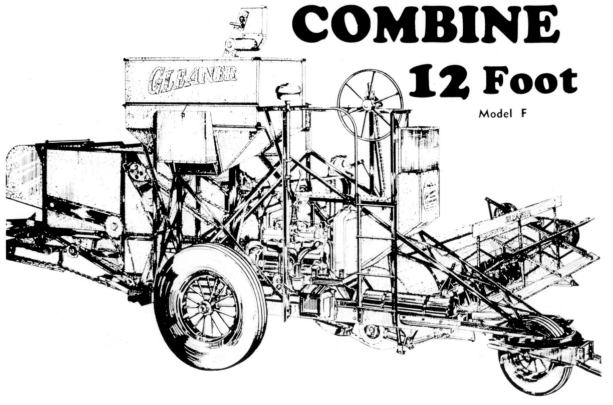

The Quality Line

Original Auger Type Combine.
Direct Feed—Auger to Cylinder.
Over 13-ft. Separating Length.
Rasp Bar Cylinder—No Grates.

Two Fans—Perfected Cleaning.
"Full Jeweled" – 70 Bearings.
Ford—Industrial Engine.
Light Draft—Easy to Operate.

MANUFACTURED BY

GLEANER HARVESTER CORPORATION
INDEPENDENCE, MO.

Left

This is the machine that set the pace in the 1930s, the celebrated Allis-Chalmers All-Crop 60. Following the introduction of this compact 5 ft cut model in 1935, it soon earned the title of the 'Corn Belt Combine'. It was also widely acclaimed as the 'successor to the binder' and played a significant part in making this machine obsolete. The All-Crop 60 originated from a design by Bob Hall and Guy Fleming. The keen eye of Allis-Chalmers' HC Merritt recognised the potential of

their machine as it was undergoing development. A deal was struck that brought it to the 'harvest capital of the world' as La Porte was then known. Two more years of hard work resulted in a combine which took the farming world by surprise when the All-Crop 60 was demonstrated in its completed form. A production run that finally ended with a special batch leaving the Essendine UK plant in 1962, speaks for itself. This B-125 powered model, owned by Stuart Gibbard, was only overshadowed by another that his

family opeated for over 20 trouble-free years

Below

In the 1940s, the combine harvester was still a relatively recent arrival in Europe. So much so that Claas issued a number of instruction bulletins to the users of the new machines. These bulletins helped the development of combine harvesting techniques. This one was issued in 1941

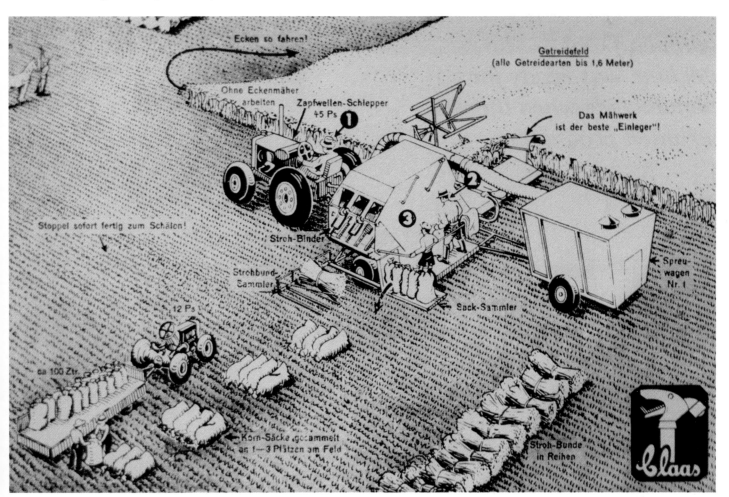

Below
Tom Carroll was appointed by Massey Harris in 1937. His brief was to develop a self-propelled combine. He produced the model 20-20A which, after some refinement, became the 21. This was the model which first introduced the word 'combine' to the world, doing away with the previous title 'reaper-thresher'. The model 21 is also famous for its participation in the American 'Harvest Brigade' operation of 1944. Five hundred model 21s were operated South to North for a distance of 1,500 miles. These machines pioneered the technique of harvesting with the season. This system is still favoured in America. The example shown is owned by Arthur Hinch of Stamford, Lincolnshire, and is housed with what is probably the largest collection of Caterpillar tractors in the UK

Below
*The late Tom Carroll was well
respected in the world of combine
harvesters. The machine he is testing
is an Eschwege built model 630 which
was equipped with a Rausendorf straw
press*

Left
*The Class Super series was introduced
in 1946. Later on the Super Junior and
Super Automatic were added to the
range. All of these were popular
machines.*

Below
A cutaway view of the Super

Above

A typical harvesting scene in the UK, circa 1947. Many pull-type combines of this period used auxiliary engines to power the cutting and threshing gear. The tractor simply pulled the harvester across the field. As more efficient tractors were developed, auxiliary engines were dispensed with and the combine was operated from a power take off on the tractor. This particular Minneapolis-Moline gave good service for many years

Above

In 1949 Massey Harris opened a new plant at Kilmarnock on the West coast of Scotland. The first models to roll off the production line were 720 series machines. These soon became highly sought after by contractors and farmers who had long been starved of an efficient means of harvesting. The late William Robertson of Laurencekirk, was one of the first to take advantage of the improved harvesting capabilities offered by the 720. He took 25 of the Massey Harris machines to the cereal fields of Lincolnshire and worked the season Northwards, following the practice favoured in America. The 720 and later 780 series vehicles featured a number of important engineering advances. Both types used unified threads and hydraulic applications more commonly seen in the aircraft industry. In 1953 Massey Harris made the opening moves in its protracted merger with the Harry Ferguson Company. This 726, the most well known model in the range, has only recently retired and countless 780's are still working on small farms

Above

Leon Claeys founded his farm machinery company in Zedelgem, Belgium, in 1906. Having been involved in the manufacture of threshing machines for a considerable time, it was a short step to move into combine production. The company's 1952 MZ, is widely credited as being the first self-propelled European combine. The 1960s saw the range extended, a change of name to Clayson and the company's acquisition by New Holland in 1964

Right

The Ransomes pull-type of 1952 was designed and built by the Bolinders-Munktell Company of Sweden but from 1953 onwards was produced under licence in Ipswich. During the late 1940s, Ransomes had an agreement with Ford to build equipment that was compatible with Fordson tractors. On the basis of this deal the FR insignia was included in the livery and advertising used for early versions of the 1952 Ransomes

Overleaf

You could be forgiven for asking what a photograph of a lorryload of scrap is doing in a book about combine harvesters. The derelict piece of machinery pictured started life as a Marshall pull-type. John and David Jolley bought it as found and are going to have their hands full restoring it. Time, effort and a little ingenuity can work wonders

Left
In 1947, Allis-Chalmers began
development work on a self-propelled
machine. In spite of having
considerable expertise, gained from
their 40 and 60 series models, this
model did not appear on the market
for almost six years. Its eventual
introduction coincided with the
acquisition of the Gleaner Baldwin
Company in 1955. The new self-
propelled model failed to live up to
expectations and never achieved the
popularity of the Corn Belt Combine,
the model 60

Previous page
It is appropriate that a picture such as
this should originate in California,
where so much important development
work was carried out during the
nineteenth century. The climate and
conditions proved ideal for combine

harvester operations and allowed
Moore, Hascall, Holt and numerous
others, to achieve much in terms of
improved design and efficiency. These
16 Massey Harris self-propelled units
were working in the Fresno area in
1953. It is a pity that a wide angle or
aerial shot was not taken at the time

Above
Rauma-Repola Rosenlow of Finland is
believed to be the largest producer of
small and medium sized combines in
the world. The company supplies other
major manufacturers with trial plot
machines, in addition to marketing its
own models. In the foreground is an
example of the company's first model,
the Sampo 657. Behind that is a Sampo
410 of 1975 vintage. The Massey-
Ferguson 8, 10, 16 and 20 trial plot
machines are all 'badge engineered'
and carry the Finnish maker's plate

Below
The sumer of 1959 was outstanding.
All the combine manufacturers
worked extremely hard to produce a
colourful and impressive display at the
annual Suffolk show. This Viking/Volvo
ST68 is accompanied by an Aktiv pull-
type model M and flanked by a Claas
on one side and a Ransomes on the
other

Right
John Beeston is the owner of this
particular Massey-Ferguson 780, seen
at work in August 1989. Beeston's 780
has given stirling service for some
years now. He anticipates many more
trouble-free seasons from this
machine which only has a small
acreage to handle

This British built, pull-type IH B64, shown at a farm sale, was quite a popular model in its day. Having seen what miracles can be wrought by a good restorer, it is certain that this machine could be saved. As a matter of interest, an updated version of this model , with a modern threshing cylinder and pick-up reel, is hopefully, going to be produced by the Alvan Blanch Development Company some time in the 1990s. It is a low cost, easy to operate machine, ideal for developing countries

Below

The Claeys M103 was a popular model. This machine, owned by the Reeves family of Adbaston, Staffordshire, was one of quite a number operated in the Eccleshall area. Bill Jackson, a local custom operator, still owns three models.

Bamfords Ltd, the well known Uttoxeter farm machinery manufacturer, imported Claeys' combines for many years. Their involvement started with the model MK and continued until New Holland took over Claeys or Clayson, as the company had become known

Left
The Ködel and Böhm firm of Lauingen, dates back to 1870. In 1936 it announced the completion of its 100,000th threshing machine. Work on the development of a combine began in 1940. This model GM 4 collected a bronze medal at the prestigious DLG show in 1958. In 1969, Ködel and Böhm became a member of the Klockner-Humbolt-Deutz AG group

Left
The operator of this Heinrich Lanz MB 18S must have been well pleased with his efforts. The Fraülein is certainly looking pleased with the sample on show!

Overleaf
Should you wish to see this machine, minus decorations, here it is again. It was equipped with a Mercedes OM 636, 32.5 hp diesel engine and a 2 m header. After being acquired by the Moline based John-Deere company in 1956, the firm of Heinrich Lanz became known as John-Deere-Lanz. The latter continued to produce and market Lanz models until new designs became available from the parent company. The John-Deere-Lanz plant at Zweibrucken was to become the centre for European harvester production in the 1960s

Left
When it was new, back in 1961, this Ransomes 902 cost £2,600. A similar sized machine today costs somewhere between £50,000 and £60,000. Last summer, as in previous years, it brought in the harvest with a minimum of downtime

Above
The Allis-Chalmers Gleaner had its first, very successful, UK trials in 1956. Remarkably, at least one is still operating. The machine in question has been owned by its original purchaser, Les Dessurne, for all of its service life. Allis-Chalmers began production in the UK at its Essendine facility in 1958. It continued there until the introduction of the model 5000 in 1969. As it turned out, this was the last new model to appear from Essendine because of the Bamford takeover of 1971. This machine was an exhibit at the 'Year of Allis-Chalmers' show, staged by the Northumberland Vintage Club in October 1988

Below

When J. Freudendahl A-S announced its range of wrap-around combines in 1961, it found the market more receptive to this concept than Claas had when it launched its own wrap-around in the 1930s. Over the next 25 years the company produced 25,000 of the two models on offer. The 'New Type' Fordson Major, seen in the background, indicates that this example is an early model.

Right

The completion of the last John Deere model 55 (opposite) self-propelled combine in 1969 marked the end of a 22 year production run. Obviously the model 55 was a very popular machine. Deere were noted for introducing the first commercially available corn head attachment in 1954

JOHN DEERE
NO. 55
Self-Propelled
COMBINE

HARVESTS MORE ACRES EVERY DAY...
SAVES MORE GRAIN AT LOWER COST

Below
With a family background of plant
breeding and agricultural research,
the Hans-Ulrich Hege Company was
ideally suited to producing trial plot
combines. It entered the market in
1964 with the Hedge 125A. This
machine was to become popular in
many countries

Right
The mid 1960s was a boom time for
both grain harvesting and the combine
industry with owner/operators
replacing their machines at short,
regular intervals. This picture shows a
wide variety of Massey-Ferguson
products including the 510 model. At
this time the series was midway
through its development and the 510
was at the height of its popularity

Overleaf
This trio of Claas Supers were
operational in Austria a long time
after their initial delivery.

Left

A trio of Cavaliers; the Ransomes type. One is to be cannibalized for spares while the other two are awaiting new owners. The last Ransomes combines were the Crusader and Cavalier models of the mid 1970s. Both were efficient and popular machines but fell victim to economic factors beyond the control of the industry. Collings Bros. of Abbotsley Ltd handled the Ransomes brand for quite a long time and still hold a substantial stock of parts

Above

Johnsons of Banks is a well known name in the North-Western agriculture and preservation scene. Long established contractors, the firm operates a fleet of six Volvo 950s.

This 4WD tractor has been custom-built using a 950's engine, wheels, steering gear and cab. It is an impressive machine. A 10 ton capacity winch is fitted and this makes it very versatile

Below
*Arbos, an Italian company, has
considerable experience with
combines and has produced a wide
rage over the years, including a
tracked model for rice operations*

Below

The model 5000 was the last combine to be built by Allis-Chalmers in the UK. In 1971 Bamfords Ltd bought A-C Farm Machinery. After the take-over the 5000 was quickly dropped in favour of Bamfords existing Volvo franchise. The combine pictured was at the Northumberland 'Year of Allis-Chalmers' event in 1988.

Right

Claas advertising has always equalled the quality of its products. This attractive and well produced brochure features the 7 ft cut Cosmos which was available during the late 1960s. The brochure quotes an option of VW, Ford, Perkins or Deutz power units

An interesting development of the late 1960s; the Fisher Humphries /Dechentrieter/Lely Victory combine with folding header. Initial machines were sourced from the Bavarian manufacturer, along with a supply of further components. Development work took place in the UK. On the later Mark III models, the ZF mechanical transmission was replaced by a Linde hydrostatic unit. Models of this type also had 14ft and 18ft headers and were fitted with Perkins engines. Subsequently Ford power units were used. Conventional Lely-Dechentrieter JD 210S and 240S, 7 ft and 8 ft 6 in. models were also offered. By the late 1970s, the combine market had contracted considerably, and Lely, after considering the vast development costs required for a limited production run machine, opted for investment in smaller higher volume products. Victory production ceased after a total of 54 units had been built. Several are still operating in the UK and Belgium

Above
A tight fit but this Victory just managed to squeeze through. Here the advantages of a folding header are obvious

Below
*A is a schematic diagram of the 760.
Massey-Ferguson are noted for a
variety of technical advances during
the 1970s, including the power flow
table and the quick-attach header*

Right
*A Massey-Ferguson 760 on test prior to
delivery to the late Mr William
Robertson. The archway it is passing
through is at Fettercairn. It was
originally built to secure a visit from
Queen Victoria, in competition with
nearby Edzell for royal attention*

Above
In 1976, the popular folk group 'The Wurzels', had a major success with their 'Combine Harvester' record. It did a lot for the band's popularity amongst the farming community as well. The Wurzels; Pete Budd, Tommy Banner and Tony Baylis, are seen here posing with a Massey-Ferguson 780 for the record's sleeve illustration

Right
1975 was obviously a good year for combine sales in Shropshire. Here we can see eleven model 1530s prepared for delivery by George Oakley Ltd, New Holland's Shrewsbury dealer

Left
*It has a 150 to 180 hp power
requirement and is obviously intended
for large scale harvesting operations.
It was designed by Herr Helwig
Schmitt, who was employed by
Massey-Ferguson at their Eschwege
plant in the early 1980s.*

Above
*Seen in transit, this combine differs
from earlier models from Baldwin,
Claas, Ferguson and JF in that it is a
'drive in' type*

Above

Laverda, a member of the Fiatagri group, has a long history of involvement in farming. The company has the capacity to produce up to 2000 combines per year. One of its models is pictured above. Self-propelled windrowers, for indirect harvesting, are another of Laverda's harvest related range

Right

A number of Allis-Chalmers model Ls in wheat. The model L was available with standard headers up to 24 ft wide and corn headers up to eight rows. At this time the MH was Allis-Chalmers' hillside offering and the model F was the smallest unit in the range

Above
A far cry from the original reapers of McCormick, Hussey and the other pioneers of the 1800s. They would have been rather perplexed had they encountered this Massey-Ferguson, 'state of the art', electronic, in-cab monitoring system

Right
Sperry New Holland was the first of the leading names to annouce a rotary design. It launched the TR (twin rotor) model 70 in 1975. At the same time the company also established a manufacturing base in America. The leading machine shown here is a TR95 of the 1979 to 1984 period

The owner of this team obviously likes green! No prizes for guessing where they were built

Above
While Perkins has been owned by
Massey-Ferguson since 1959, the
company has been producing engines
since the 1930s. It has built over ten
million units of which some five
million are still in operation. Gardner
and Rolls-Royce Diesels are both
owned by Perkins

Right
This Deere Titan 8820 should have no
problems driving over soft ground on
its floatation tyres

The 1980s were a very difficult time for the farm machinery business. Over capacity and ultra high interest rates were just two of the problems which dogged the industry. Mergers, buyouts and a host of trading and manufacturing agreements brought about considerable changes with more to come. White Farm Equipment and Avco New Idea are two long-standing names affected by these events

Above
Claas UK Ltd (J Mann) modified a large number of the compact 25 and 30 models for research station work. The example shown is one of a mixed fleet of specialist machines, operated by the National Institute of Agricultural Botany at their various UK locations

Right
A tidy looking Fortschritt E516 awaiting a new owner. The combine's header has been removed, for transportation, and placed on the trailer to the left of the vehicle. When introduced in the 1970s, this model was claimed to have the largest threshing cylinder area of any machine available at the time

Left
*A corn/maize header options from
Arbos SpA*

Above
*Arbos SpA leave no one in any doubt of
what its hillside models can do*

Left

*They do things big in Texas. Well,
they have to, it is a big place.
Seventeen Deeres at work during 1983*

Right

*There can be no doubt what IH have to
offer, looking at this brochure*

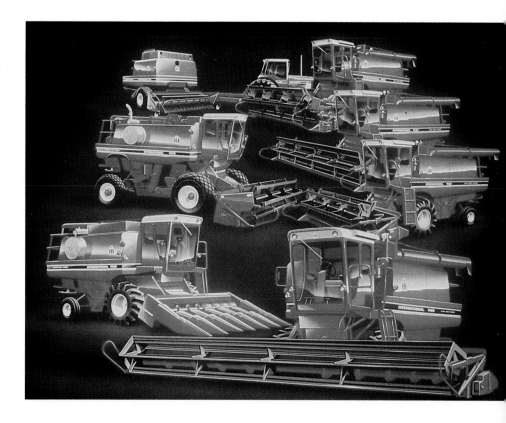

Above
An IH Axial flow at work in scenic surroundings

Right
Farming correspondent and broadcaster, Keith Stevens, inspecting the New Holland 8030 at the 'British Food and Farming Year' show. The event was staged at the Swynnerton Heath farm, courtesy of Lord Stafford

Below

The giant Rostelmach plant came online in 1932, producing S-1 pull-type models. The main components used in their manufacture were similar to those of the Communar but a larger header size and other improvements were incorporated. The S4 and S6 self-propelled models appeared in the late 1940s. Continual upgrading through the years that followed resulted in the 1971 Niva range. These had a very comprehensive specification including electronic grain loss monitors. In 1986, the Rostelmach plant began production of the Don-1500. These differ from their Western counterparts in their use of a fixed concave anduniversal rotors

Below
A report from a farm machinery expert, who briefly viewed an example on display at a trade fair, suggests that these are well designed and constructed machines. This one is intended for use in the 'Black Earth' regions of the USSR. The soil there is very light and porous. Using tracked vehicles with curved links helps to prevent soil damage

Overleaf
In late 1978, Allis-Chalmers entered the rotary market with its N5, 6 and 7 models. These differed from the rotary combines of other manufacturers in that the cylinder was mounted transversely to give a 'natural flow' effect. This N6 is pictured with a K2, the smallest unit in Allis-Chalmers conventional range

Above
The Klockner-Humholt-Deutz AG
group took over Allis-Chalmers in May
1985. The company then became know
as Deutz-Allis. Today, the R40, 50, 60
and 70 rotary models are the main
products manufactured at the
Independence plant in Missouri

Right
The Shelbourne Reynolds Oilseed Rape
Swather is a typical machine of the
type. Both the Shelbourne Reynolds
2000 and 2100 models use base
machines supplied by Fortschritt. The
Canadian McDon unit, shown
opposite, was purpose built for the
indirect harvesting of cereal crops

Indirect harvesting is popular in America and elsewhere. It involves cutting and swathing the crop before it is picked up and threshed by a combine equipped with a pickup reel. This reduces the problems caused by wind damage and weed infestation

Left
A Laverda on a typical sidehill operation

Above
A rotary type Massey-Ferguson/White threshing cylinder

Left

And this Deere Titan II looks equally at home harvesting on a sidehill

Above

A Deutz Fahr M660. One of several which were converted for trial plot use by the Coleman Engineering (Machinery) Company Ltd. This company currently imports Sampo Rosenlow 130 and 580 model trial plot machines from Finland. Shown opposite is a 580 with a 3.97 m table and an 84 hp Valmet DL 411 engine

The Fortschritt E512 is the smallest of the company's current range. The example seen here is equipped with a two row pickup reel for threshing from the swath. Another interesting attachment produced by this company is its crop wall sensor which maintains a full cut to ensure maximum productivity

Above
Ever since the earliest days of mechanisation fire has been the chief enemy of the combine harvester. Even with today's technology it is still a problem

Right
The sun canopy is the clue to the location of this shot. Massey-Ferguson S.A, Brazil, designed the 3640 with some assistance from Eschwege. Power is provided by a 6.357 Perkins diesel

Below
The SIMA show in Paris, staged each March, attracts the latest in farm machinery, this Bourgnon Axiale being just one exhibit among many. The number of combine manufacturers now left barely reaches double figures, so it is quite a change to see something different

Right and below
Kilmarnock no longer produces the big red machines but important development work on Massey-Ferguson's 'Whole Crop Harvester' still goes on there. The Whole Crop Harvester is designed for areas where the stalks are also used for foodstuffs. It is a compact, tractor-mounted machine which is relatively easy to use and is capable of operating in the stationary role.

Left
*The latest developments by Claas
includes the Maxi, an addition to the
Dominator range. The Maxi
incorporates extra power, increased
grain tank capacity and heavier duty
axles and wheels. An agreement with
Caterpillar also gives the interesting
option of machines equipped with
Caterpillar's patented rubber track
system*

Above
*Visitors to the Claas dealer convention
at Hersewinkel in 1989 might have
wondered if their eyes were playing
tricks on them. It is not every day you
see a flying combine harvester*

Below
One of the smallest rotary combines must be this AMX 1600 manufactured by Cicoria SrL of Italy. The company also produces two-wheeled threshers which are driven by power-take-off.

Cicoria's new AMX 2000 has a variety of interesting features. The vehicle comes in both two and four-wheel-drive configurations and acts as a carrier for a number of different equipment packages. The harvesting apparatus consists of a conventional cutting bar, mounted on a height adjustable platform. This works in conjunction with a 2 m, variable speed, axial awner and a reverse awner, made of interchangeable sections for threshing different materials. A new type of rotary cleaning system is fitted which allows the AMX 2000 to operate on steep ground without the need for self-levelling mechanisms

Below
*The Hege company now offer a full
range of machines for crop research
operations; plot drills, tool carriers
and static threshers to name but a
few. The 140 is the medium sized
model of the range*

Left
Another attachment from Shelbourne Reynolds Engineering Ltd – the Combine Vertical Knife. It is hydraulically driven and is a boon in heavily tangled crops

Below
1989 may not have been a good year for yields but it was certainly a good year for breaking harvesting records. Using a Deere 1177 Turbo, kindly loaned by P Tuckwell Ltd, the Tendring Hundred Young Farmers Club set a field-to-table record of 26 minutes and 37 seconds. Their secret weapon was a baker's oven strategically located in the field. Knowing the competitive spirit of young farmers, it is doubtful if this record will last very long

Left
This record concerns conventional harvesting. It goes to Phillip Baker and his family who farm 750 acres in Oxfordshire. 165 tons of drought hit Galahad wheat went into the bin between 10 am and 6 pm, aided by two eight ton trailers for on-the-move unloading

Right
Brochure for SRE's SR2000 Rape Swather

A cutaway White 9720/Massey-Ferguson 8590. In 1989 Massey-Ferguson's North American division bought the Canadian White Corporation. After the buy-out, Massey-Ferguson continued to market the White 9720 rotary model but also offered this machine in its own livery, under the model number 8590. Since this exercise in badge engineering, Massey-Ferguson has re-vamped its policy in North America and its combines are now produced by the Western Combine Corporation and Claas

Left and overleaf
This Stripper Header Attachment, developed recently by the Shelbourne Reynolds Company, set a new record for unconventional harvesting when it was attached to a Ford New Holland TF46, owned by Barton Farms of Gainsborough, Lincolnshire. The 6 m header harvested 306.52 tons of Fortress wheat (13.09% moisture) in 7 hours 34 minutes and 19 seconds. (The actual machine is seen on the back cover)